Star Wars is finally telling women
cross out everybody
to start enjoying The Thing

for Sjaak
who makes the best Huttese slime pods in the Galaxy

STAR WARS IS FINALLY TELLING WOMEN * CROSS OUT * EVERYBODY TO START ENJOYING THE THING

2018 - 2019

The full name of my creativity coach Sara,
is Sara Saltee.
www.salteeacademy.com

First edition
© 2021
All rights reserved.

ISBN 978-1-716-27780-1

available at lulu.com
written under pseudonym LS Harteveld
cover photo Katrina Cooper-Hinton
somerandomchick.picfair.com

www.lsharteveld.nl
Twitter @LSHarteveld

Rey:
"People keep telling me they know me. But no one does."

Ben Solo:
"But I do."

final trailer for
The Rise Of Skywalker (2019)

"But I do"
was not in the movie

1

STAR WARS IS FINALLY TELLING WOMEN *CROSS OUT* EVERYBODY TO START ENJOYING THE THING

Star Wars is a movie franchise currently on its eighth episode. And what "The Thing" is?

Okay, you know what The Thing is right?

One of the Reylo accounts I follow on Twitter had put out a poll on what we viewed as signs of the collapse of civilization, and she additionally tweeted;

"I wanted to add "Telling women they shouldn't enjoy The Thing" but that's been happening for eons."

That's where I got the idea.

Reylos are a community who support the story line in the latest Star Wars trilogy that Rey, a good girl from the deserted planet Jakku, will fall in love with dark side warrior Kylo Ren or with "Ben Solo" his original name- before he passed over to the dark side.

Rey's official Star Wars bio says, and to me (a Reylo) every word in this sentence is hot;

"She was captured by the dark side warrior Kylo Ren."

The interrogation scene between Kylo Ren and Rey is important for the story. As soon as Kylo Ren takes off his mask, she can't take her eyes off him. Then he invades her mind, using The Force, and he says;

"Don't be afraid, I feel it too."

He is referring to The Force – which he uses for supernatural powers. But right now he can feel The Force between the two of them. Connecting them.
She has always known "something" was inside of her, and she had Han and Maz briefly explaining what "the Force" was – just the general idea. But she hasn't connected their explanations to what she feels inside of her.

"But now it's awake," she says about the power inside of her.

During the interrogation scene, due to Kylo Ren interrogating her with the Force, she learns how to use it for the very first time.
And intrudes his mind in return.

He leaves the room immediately, reporting to his Master, Snoke. Before capturing Rey and before the interrogation scene, Snoke has already asked Kylo;
"There has been an awakening. Have you felt it?"
And Kylo answered: "Yes".

The interrogation scene is the first time Rey learns how to use the force, yet both Kylo and Snoke have sensed Rey's awakening days before.
You know what happened, days before?
And what (most likely) caused the awakening?
Kylo was on Jakku.

Just for a brief moment, but his presence there was powerful enough to awaken the Force in Rey.

She sensed it. She sensed him. And suddenly this thing called "the Force" was awake in her.
The first female lead character in a Star Wars movie, who uses Force powers, had them awakened by a tall warrior, covered in flowing black robes, setting foot on her planet.

And she learned to use them, not by receiving any formal education like all the Jedis before her, but just by being tied to an interrogation chair by Kylo Ren and having him kneeling before her saying in his sultry voice;
"You're my guest."

That's how this girl learns.

Those scenes tell you that the Force, for this trilogy, is connected to the dynamics between Rey and Kylo.
Not to the relationship of an apprentice with his Master.

Ever since The Force Awakens came out in 2015 there has been much debate over the fact if Reylos are right, if there even is a romantic story line between the two, but that's another discussion and one I'm not particularly interested in.
For me it's blatantly obvious that Rey and Kylo Ren are in love with each other.
And judging by how gorgeous Kylo Ren looks, I'm convinced Disney feels exactly the same way.

So that's not what this piece is about.

This article is about what makes the story line so compelling. What makes this Star Wars saga entirely different from its predecessors, and especially the use of The Force.

And again, I'm not talking about if you can fly through space using the force, or bi-locate yourself using it.
Which were things that have been speculated on if this was realistic (???) and if they should have been in the movies.
No, I'm talking about the fact that if you watch the two movies The Force Awakens and The Last Jedi, you can see something entirely new added to the equation.

Sex.

And not to make babies.

The "romantic tension" between Rey and Kylo Ren, as Mark Hamill the actor who plays Luke Skywalker put it, is only half of it.
The other half, is sexual tension.
And it's precisely this sexual tension that is going to glue the entire thirty year old saga together.

Traditionally, so that means the first six episodes of the saga, The Force was used by the good guys, the spiritual warriors called the Jedi, and by the dark side, The Sith.
But the latest trilogy is said to take an entirely different approach.

That of the middle, of gray.

It's based on the notion that there can never be peace (balance) if we keep thinking in terms of good and bad.
We have to accept the dark side of life, in each other, but also in ourselves. It is just as disturbing to believe you're entirely good and

clean, as it is disturbing to believe you're a power driven monster who doesn't need love.

That is the story of the third trilogy.

Back to Rey and Kylo Ren.

In the light of the theme of the third trilogy, their romantic story line represents the merging of the good (Rey) and the bad (Kylo Ren).

We also get to know Kylo Ren's soft side in The Last Jedi (the light within the dark) and we get to learn a bit about the aggression that resides in Rey.

Although for someone who watches the roaring rampage of revenge Kill Bill about twenty times a year, as I do, it is not that obvious.
But I'm taking other people's word for it, that her fighting skills are rooted in aggression and that she seems to take pleasure in knocking people in the head.

So within light Rey, we have a hint of her darkness.
And within dark Kylo we can see the light shining through.
Rey and Kylo Ren are like yin and yang; each possesses a part of the other.

This new and improved vision on balance between the light and the dark, is also symbolized in the first Jedi temple on the island of Ahch-to.
This temple holds the old Jedi texts – which will prove that the original Force users were gray, not good or bad.
And the temple itself also contains the light; a tree above the ground containing the books.

And the darkness – a cold dark hole in the ground and sucks you into its waters and then scares the shit out of you with a mirrored cave where you are all alone with your greatest fear.

The tree, representing the "safe" cerebral wisdom of the Jedi, can be destroyed.

But the cave is inscrutable, and way more solid, being made from the sea and the rock that makes the island.

Luke is training Rey, and he's instructing her how to meditate on the Force.

In her vision, she sees the big (dare we say "hairy"? Because it is!) hole in the ground, the cave under the island.
It is calling her.
She moves towards it, ignoring Luke shouting her not to.

The hole erupts into a giant fountain, as if it comes from underneath her. From the rock on which she is sitting.
A giant fountain, entering at her pelvis, and squirting up high into the sky.
She is knocked down by the strength of it, flings her eyes open, and wakes up lying down. Soaked. And shocked.

But not as much as Luke, who looks at her, appalled.
"I've seen this raw strength only once before. In Ben Solo."

A "raw strength", that Ben Solo possesses?
And that was awakened in Rey, by Ben Solo's presence?
That sweeps her off her feet, leaves her wet and exhausted, and uncle Luke appalled?
And then Luke basically explaining what just happened to her, by attributing the power she just experienced to his nephew Ben?

But let's not jump to conclusions.

Let's just, for a minute more, assume that Uncle Luke was referring to the dark side of the Force as it was portrayed in episodes 1-6;
as a desire for universal domination, a possessive kind of love and the use of supernatural powers for your own personal hunger to control life and the people around you.

Uncle Luke was just concerned about Rey becoming Darth Rey and plunging the world into darkness and despair.

Next story.

It is nighttime on Ahch-to.

Rey has given in to her desire to explore what's in the hole, and she has gone out to see what answers the cave could give her.
She's disappointed with its cryptic answers, and feels terribly lonely.

By now she and Kylo Ren, or Ben Solo, are being connected by the Force regularly. It's like Skype, just that the other person can actually be seen and experienced in the flesh with you.

And also – they don't control it.
They can't dial each other up if they want to. The Force seems to connect them unintentionally. Although that too, is not true. If you look closer.

Before their first ever Force bond, Kylo was sitting in the medical wing and had his wounds attended to by a droid. Wounds that she inflicted. So he was probably already thinking about her.

In the scene above, she had just risked her life going straight into the darkness of the cave well only to be terribly disappointed and lonely. And there you go:

* Forcebond pops up*

"You are not alone," Kylo says to the disappointed Rey.

"Neither are you," she says.

And slowly she reaches her hand towards him.

Kylo Ren takes off his thick leather glove. Slowly.
His master Snoke has been invading his mind from before he was born. Even when he was physically still with his parents, he already had this evil abuser inside his own head, corrupting him.
Demeaning him.

Switching over to the dark side was probably a relief for Kylo; at least his surroundings now matched his inner world.
But it was a world without love.

Kylo has never felt love in his life.

He reaches his bare hand to her. It is trembling. Her hand is steady, but his.. yes. There is a tremble. Their fingertips meet.
The Force theme from John Williams sets in.

You get the idea right?
And do you know what Luke does when he barges in on the two?

HE BLOWS UP THE HUT!

Now does that seem to you like he would do that because;

a. Kylo is raping and beating Rey and about to kill her?

or

b. because Luke is a jealous old hermit who can't stand the idea of Rey having sex, and especially not with his evil nephew Kylo Ren who by the way he, Luke, was supposed to train and make a good man of, but failed miserably?

Cock blocker Luke, we Reylos call him.

Or at least I do.

But not without acknowledging that Mark Hamill is both the nicest celebrity on Twitter, as well as the most heroic and epic character in The Last Jedi.

So no hard feelings.

But keeping Rey from her first night of experiencing making love, and Kylo from his first experience of being loved – that was a horrible thing to do. Even more unforgivable as betraying Ben Solo and giving him up to the dark side.

THIS WAS YOUR CHANCE TO SET THINGS RIGHT

Okay, I'll stop yelling at Luke.

Because there was actually a point in bringing this up. Aside from the point that the force bond between Kylo and Rey is absolutely not just a romantic one, but a sexual one.

Because Rey represents the light sight of the force – love.

But the thing that sparked it, that ignited The Force in her, was not love. Because Rey was a loving person all throughout her life. And although the Force has been there, inside of her, it was only sparked when someone who she would become sexually interested in set foot on Jakku.

And it is this aspect of the Force that Luke is afraid of.

He's not afraid Rey will plunge the world into darkness. He's afraid she'll become sexually active with Kylo Ren. That is the dark side, Luke is warning her for.
That is the "raw strength" that is connecting the two.

Raw strength is a referral to sex. Not to love.

A lot of people think the new Star Wars trilogy will be about Love conquering all. I can understand that, but

a. there has always been a lot of love between light side users. And this has never conquered anything. Yes, love has brought Darth Vader to the light, but that story has already been told.

b. Love being the key clearly doesn't support the Gray Jedi idea, and the merging of dark and light. In my opinion they can only make Love conquer all the moral of the saga if they see Love as being the light dot, in the dark half of the Yin and Yang symbol.

But it doesn't explain the dark dot in the white half of the Yin and Yang symbol.

Because that dot? That's sex.

c. And the third reason I feel there is way more behind the Rey-Kylo Ren story line than a simple Romeo and Juliet theme is that Love is not a power that would scare the shit out of Luke Skywalker. Love is not the "raw strength", about which he says;

"It didn't scare me enough then. It does now."

That is sex.

Rey is the first character in the Star Wars movies, with whom the dark side of the Force is (to me at least) only apparent in her sexual power. Like I said, I can't see her going on a rampage of revenge, nor do I see her becoming a cruel empress of the galaxy.

Which leaves only one option – her raw strength, is a sexual one. The key that awaked the Force in her.

For Kylo though, things are a bit different.

He has not known love, which is why his hand was trembling touching Rey, and he's very familiar with the dark side of the force in terms of being mentally abused (by Snoke) and inevitably turning cold hearted and cruel himself.

Kylo is probably not a virgin.

He's ten years older than Rey and his whole body language – especially in The Force Awakens – radiates that he's highly comfortable in his own body.

The way he fights Finn at the end of The Force Awakens – swinging his light saber, showing his physical dominance in a cocky, totally non-functional manner that is clearly connected to him being jealous of Finn.
Not to using the most effective way to take out an opponent.
That fighting style just tells that he enjoys being in his body, and that

he knows how to move it.
Especially when he wants to show his sexual superiority.

And also; watch how Rey, on the other hand, fights clumsily because she's holding a light saber (!!) for the first time in her life.

And don't forget the ending where Kylo, sparing her life and not playing at his full strength because he knows it's her first time and he fancies her, offers Rey the opportunity to learn from him how to use the Force and the saber.

"You need a teacher! I can show you the ways of the Force!"
Kylo shouts to Rey.

As Luke would say;
"Amazing. Every word in that sentence, was wrong."

Because as soon as Kylo mentions the Force, Rey suddenly remembers everything Han and Maz told her about the Force, and what she experienced with Kylo in the interrogation chair.

The strength between them that Kylo referred to as;
"Don't be afraid. I feel it too."

She murmurs; "The Force?"
Suddenly remembering all of it. She meditates there, right in the middle of wrestling Kylo. She taps into the strength, swings out from underneath him, and rocks that light saber like a pro.

Soon the mighty Kylo Ren is on his back, covered in wounds she inflicted.
"Beaten by a girl who never held a light saber in her life," as Snoke would remind Kylo, in the next movie Last Jedi.

From what Star Wars has shown us so far we can conclude that Kylo Ren represents the dark side of the yin and yang symbol.
And the light dot within him, within the dark half of life, is love.
Represented by his romantic love for Rey.

And Rey is the light side of the yin and yang symbol. She represents all people who like being good, loyal, clean, and reminds us that we can be more than that.
That there is a Force within us, that has always been there.
And not so much what, or how, but who will awaken that Force.

The Force will be impossible to miss, if it is taken out of its dormant state.
Don't worry, we'll feel it too.

And that it will be so fascinating, and calling us, that the only thing that makes sense is to answer the call and to jump into the cave of the unknown, to explore it.
And yes, you must be prepared to come out disappointed.
There will be no easy answers.

But the person who sparked your Force, whose presence you felt from half a planet away.
The one who "felt it too" and who told you not to be afraid?
That person will be waiting for you, when you come out.

To complete your own saga.

*Star Wars is finally telling women *cross out* everybody to start enjoying The Thing #reylo*
was written on 28 January 2018

2

THE THING VERSUS THE THINGS
A CRASH COURSE PRIORITIZING
ILLUSTRATED WITH REYLO

Just how this post came about illustrates the difference between THE THING and The Things.
I have a to-do list for today, but instead of taking care of that I'm here.
Behind my computer at six thirty P.M. with a glass of wine.
Pushing back my schedule, on which I'm already seriously behind, for at least another sixty minutes.

Because writing, more often than not, simply hijacks the day. Or in this case the evening.
Which is why I always repress the urge to do it (write for pleasure).

And today I was successful.

I had my pink desk time in the morning (playing with my notebooks and listening to inspirational videos for hours) but I also did my most important and "worldly", task:
to redo and catch up with the online part of my program for the yoga studio.

I had intended to do that for weeks, but since I had a mental break down and was happy to even be able to teach, I had put it off. So today I made it a priority to get this (reboot the online program) done.

Congratulations Miss Harteveld.

Except with the returning of my strengths, something else returned too. Which is the need to write. For the past couple of weeks I have made a meager one-Facebook-post-a-week.
But that too, is now changing. Repressing the urge to write will become more difficult by the day.

It will turn into a force to be reckoned with.
Which is exactly what it used to be before The Acute Depression.

I basically lost my will to live after Max died.
That's what it felt like anyway. I'm not going to diagnose myself but I had conversations where I reassured people that I wasn't going to kill myself.
The fact that I even felt compelled to say that, and that it was met with a sigh of relief, indicates I was far from my usual passionate self.

So I'm very glad that's over, but those weeks did have one unexpected benefit.
I didn't have my day hijacked by writing.

And when I did feel like writing, I had plenty of time, because I had lowered my expectation to zero as far as my other obligations or self-care regiment went. All the time in the world.

Yesterday I composed a post of the few diary entries I did make, that dark month.

To live up to the title of this current how-to post, *THE THING versus The Things, A crash course prioritizing illustrated with Reylo,* I'm now going to break it down and illustrate what your THING is, versus what Your Things are.

And I'll throw in some "Reylo" which, for those who don't know what that is, Reylos are the Star Wars fans in favor of Rey and Kylo Ren getting a relationship.

First: "The Things"

"The Things" can be recognized by being urgent, pressing, accumulating, status-giving. They're important by any, if not all, worldly standards.
In my little example here, "The Things" was taking care of the content for the online program.

Do note that when you're feeling totally crap, f.e. depressed, and are not able to do The Things, and that this will cause you to feel guilty. Even when you would have a permission slip from your doctor that you're mentally ill, and should ab-so-lute-ly NOT bother yourself with The Things?

You're STILL going to feel guilty for not doing The Things.

That's because they're The Things. That's what they do. That's how you can recognize them. Feel guilty for not doing them? Immediately put them on pile number two.
Labeled "The Things".

In the case of Reylo, the relationship between Rey and Kylo Ren, when he asks her to join him on a worldly level, to reign the galaxy? The scene where he reaches out his black gloved hand?

That is Kylo offering her The Things. He's offering her success by worldly standards. Rey would become an empress or queen or whatever Kylo and her would redub leadership of the First Order. She would become a mother, most likely to the heir of Kylo's throne.

She would be Somebody. When first she was literally Nobody.

That's another aspect of "The Things"; they're outcome focused. They are aimed at attaining or acquiring a certain result.

There is this high profile meme, that a lot of people use on a day-to-day basis:
"What would you do if you could not fail?"
It's supposed to inspire people to go for their dreams.

When in reality?
There is a much more powerful meme, exactly opposite to that;
"What would you do if everything you did would fail?" (by worldly standards)

If nothing would make you money. If you would not be able to hold on to any job, not make any endeavor a success. No relationship, no project. Nothing you would do would give you anything sustainable nor validation from the outside world.

THEN what would you do?

Because that?

That's THE THING!

In my case it is writing. In my low of being depressed I wondered where my rock bottom was for bouncing back, making money, taking care of myself. I assessed it was at paying my dental bill, getting dental care. If I would have to live not being able to do that, I would get myself back on my feet.

But now that I'm passionate again, and feel alive, I know it's also writing. I would always want to write. Preferably on a computer, but in a notebook if I have to.

Even if I would have to rise early to go to that normal job, to pay for those dentist bills, I would still get up and write at 5 A.M., to nourish myself on a soul level, to feel alive.

And with Reylo, the relationship between Rey and Kylo?

For them being together without achieving any results, is THE THING. With Kylo taking the risk of losing his position within the First Order, and Rey possibly having to break ties with the resistance.

In episode 8 General Leia Organa, Kylo's mother, was head of the resistance. So chances of Rey being declared persona non-grata based on her relationship with Kylo were slim.

But in 9? Who knows.

Finn and Poe, the male runners up within the rebellion, may not be so forgiving when she hooks up with what they perceive as the number one nemesis of the free people.

Within the Reylo community there is consensus that when Rey and Kylo's hand touch in the hut, in a Force vision (Kylo's not "really" there) the energy of this hand reaching scene is entirely different from the "Join me" (to rule the galaxy) scene. The most notable difference is that Kylo took his glove off in the hut.

In this scene they touch for reasons that are THE THING.

Connection.

Curiosity.

Destiny.

Desire.

Kylo Ren answering Rey's invitation to touch hands is not bringing either one of them status, it was not on their to do list, and they do not touch out of obligatory guilt.

If they had not done it, if Rey had not taken the chance to reach out, or if Kylo had not bothered to return the invitation, they would not have felt guilty.

It would have felt far worse:

As if they had deprived themselves of something.

As if they had missed their calling, because they had rejected or ignored someone who had moved them to the bone. Missed out on the one who could very well be the most important person in their lives.

Because that's the biggest difference between on one side "The Things" – the urgent, accumulating tasks and the worldly rewards attached to them. And on the other had THE THING; the spontaneous, eruptive calling of the heart and your soul wanting to do something.

The Things are rewarding by worldly standards.

But THE THING is what will give you the sensation of being alive, of having your foundations shaken, emotions violently flaring up. If you have anything, or anyone, you can't say no to? Even if it resulted in absolutely nothing aside from the experience itself?

That's THE THING.

Those are THE THINGS. Plural because you can have multiple passions, fascinations, more things that make your heart beat faster.

And after three hours and three glasses of wine, I can assure you that each of those passions is worth burning your entire to-do list for.

THE THING versus The Things
A crash course prioritizing illustrated with Reylo
was written on 14 March 2018

3

REDEMPTION

*This blogpost is about a breakup, after a 5 year long forbidden affair
to a handsome man, strong on the dark side of the Force.*

It's written to my creativity coach Sara.
Before our call I always give her a headsup.

Dear Sara,

I feel kind of nervous writing this.
As if it is The Letter of Letters, about The King of Kings and the ending
of a saga that has changed the world.
Or at least me.
But maybe it is easier to compare it to Star Wars 9, which will be
released in a couple of days.

Star Wars 9 is the final movie of the Skywalker Saga, which was started
by George Lucas over 40 years ago. It is now owned by Disney, who try
to work the material in a way that satisfies the fans without fucking it
up and disappointing everyone.
So far predictions for 9 are that they're fucking it up disappointing
everyone.

Maybe that explains why I feel Mr.Big and me have done an absolutely
amazing job ending our 5 year long affair.
We did not fuck it up.
And we have not disappointed anybody, which wasn't too hard since
nobody knew in the first place.

I think even we did not expect something that was forged into existence against the odds, against anything we had envisioned or hoped for ourselves, something which has derailed both our lives, probably more than we have realized when it was still happening; That something like that could be ended in such a loving, supportive way.

We had a breakup that was was so good, you could have built a marriage onto it and live happily ever after.

And it wasn't even my idea

So first off, I had not intimately seen him in five months.

We had kept in touch, and have seen each other at least once coincidentally; but there was nothing unusual about the way we had been interacting.

Except that five months not seeing each other in private, was longer that it had ever been.

I leave 95% of the initiative as to when we see each other to him, and in 100% of the cases I leave the initiative of longer dates, or a more intimate setting, up to him.

So when I asked him if he would like to see each other, and he suggested coffee in a public place around 2, there was nothing unusual about it.

I was guessing it would be a get-acquainted again date. And that we'd meet "properly" in days, weeks. But certainly in 2019.

So I did not expect this to be a breakup conversation, and strangely enough I am convinced that neither did he.

I think he really gave himself permission to either postpone it, or to contemplate a little more, feel into the whole vibe of what we had. Did it really needed saying?

And if so, did it need to be now?

Just like our dates had always been open and lighthearted, and our sexual play was never in the foreground until we were both warmed up to the idea, and time and location permitted it;

This final date, which could have ended in a traumatizing breakup for both parties, was so in tune that it possessed a certain beauty, intimacy.

It must have benefited from our ability to tune into each other, and to speak about something which on the surface must have looked like a disturbing topic to others – but that was supported by a deep understanding.

In the same way our sex had contained lots of powerplay and mindgames, but no safe words, no rules, something other people would judge to be irresponsible, but for us it was entirely safe,

we didn't need words to understand each other.

Our conversation merely explained the details, of why he wanted to break up and why I understood that. But our words were not used to communicate on a deeper level.

That was the same wordless bond it had always been.

When I conduct one story from what he has told me, together with what I have instinctively been feeling (remind me to get back to that), this is the story why we're breaking up:

In August I could already feel him pulling away from me.

I was doing very, very badly.

From (I think) halfway July to halfway November, I had the worst four months of my life. And the final smackdown of a 16 month period, which started July 2018.

Oh screw that about me getting back and explaining later, what I had instinctively been feeling! It's so obvious!

Months ago I wrote you a letter which contained the wise words: "Sara, whenever I'm feeling bad, please remind me that it's always about a man. And if it's not about a man, it's still about a man."

Unfortunately "Being about a man" – although it had sounded simple enough – has proven to be a complex, layered process, with the following elements.
Which probably take place in three different time zones or realities!

1. I will fall in love with a new man but not know it/ not be aware of it;

2. I will focus and stress over my writing, my publishing, my yoga or coaching business, and come up and start countless new plans and projects. None of which make me feel any better.

3. Sudden bursts of anxiety at strange moments.

4. Suicidal thoughts related to having to get a real job (and not having ample time to write)

All four things have happened both last year, as well as halfway July-half November this year.
However, the key is that I've always felt that "I was not alone". That there was something going on with him, in his life, that was influencing my reality.
Like a glitch in the Matrix.

Sometimes I was even able to pinpoint it later on, when we met within a week or so, after some major shift had happened.
And he mentioned something, and it turned out to be the moment I had felt something.
If I would have to put a model to it, I would say all four things are related to him not doing well, or related to him deliberately turning away from me.
If he's unconsciously pulling back or if his life is exciting and fun, I do not seem to have these strong responses.
But anyway, because this is all so complex, I do not blame myself for trying to solve my life by tackling individual problems.

My fear of a contract job.
My crushes with new men.
My anxiety.
How else would I be able to deal with them?

I can't call my lover and yell:
"Hey, dude, fix your life! I'm getting really bad vibes over here."

So if I combine everything he told me about why he wants to break up, with everything I have subconsciously been picking up, I would say he already started turning away within a month after our last encounter. And the explanation I got was that he finds it hard that we only share the good times together.
Which became even more pressing when something private happened.

Within months after our wonderful encounter in July, the entire situation had changed so much – first intentionally and then unintentionally – that it had become out of the question that he would still be seeing his secret mistress.
He took full responsibility, and acknowledged, that he had been turning away before that though. And did not hide behind the new situation.
I appreciated that.

But nevertheless, it did offer a very clear image that this was not something we were going to debate, or investigate. Of course we were going to breakup.
No questions asked, I would even say.
But nevertheless, it did surprise me that my whole world did not fall apart, in the hours and days after. How was this even possible?
It was like a tremendous burden had been lift from my shoulders.
I was free... but from what?

At first I could not believe it, as you can imagine. I thought there was simply no way it was going to be "this easy". But when hours turned into days, and I'm now almost at the one week marker – I can really say:

I am okay.

And there are probably a multitude of reasons for that but the two I want to highlight are:

I already did my time, and during our relationship I was feeling unsafe.

Firstly, I did my time (like in probation)

It has been 5 months since we last had sex.

That's as if you're addicted to cigarettes, get pneumonia, and by the time you're healed you have not smoked for two weeks. If you quit then, it will be a lot easier because you've already been nicotine free for two weeks.

It's the same with this relationship:

It's been five months since we've been intimate.

That's totally different to if it had been five days or even five weeks. I've already put in my time. More than that. They were the worst months of my entire life. It was the dramatic "four month smackdown", maybe meltdown would be a better word, where I looked everywhere to find an explanation for why I was feeling so bad.

I have come to terms with this breakup, without knowing what was going on.

No wonder I'm not crying now.

I've cried for four months.

The second reason:

I've always felt unsafe.

During those five years I've presented myself as the mistress of a married business man (or banker) with children, and I suggested there were difficulties within that family or marriage, which could explain both his need for fun (me) as well as why he was loyal to them and would never leave them.

But the truth was a lot more complicated than that.

And the consequences if it ever came out, were entirely different from "just" him having to fight for custody. If it came out, it could have consequences *for me*.

We had a secret affair because of him, and I supported that.

It's one of the things I can recommend to any mistress, any partner: play on his team. Don't push your own agenda, but make what's important to them, important to you.

It's the reason it worked, all those years.

And it's the reason I let him go, the minute he wants to leave. Of course I do.

But what I had failed to see, was how much the secrecy had been to protect myself. And how much anxiety it has caused. Just the thought of what might happen if it would come out, could make me sick to my stomach.

And it often did.

That's all over now. It will slowly fade into the background, and every year that passes I will be safer. I made it.

I will never go there again.

Sure; Keeping a relationship a secret for my own pleasure? Avoid all the questions, the outer justification, the expectations and all the normality?

That's one thing.

But to feel unsafe for 5 years, that was very straining.

And it was the reason I did not crash and burn when he broke up with me.

I was getting my life back.

There are speculations about Star Wars 9. And all endings so far seem to agree that Kylo Ren gets redeemed and becomes Ben Solo again. And then he dies.

None of the endings that have leaked, suggest that Rey and Kylo Ren/Ben Solo will live happily ever after.

It seems a given, that they will not.

In some versions, Kylo Ren just falls into a pit "never to be seen again". In others he has a speech, words of wisdom, and consciously sacrifices his life to save Rey, before he falls into the pit.

Star Wars 9 will end with Rey being all alone on a desert planet, with no one who understands her.

There is no happy ending and she's exactly where she started in 2015, just like I am.

Just an entirely different person.

Redemption
was written on 16 December 2019

4

A REYLO FAIRY TALE ON THE RISE OF SKYWALKER

Christmas Eve, 2019

INTRODUCTION TO THE STORY

Four hours ago, I sat down in order to write a compassionate review of The Rise of Skywalker. Something that would uplift the hearts of everyone who had been disappointed in any way shape or form, by the final episode of the saga.

And this included the people who had worked on it for all those years, and director JJ Abrams.

I was convinced that if I could look at JJ Abrams with the same compassion I had given the villain of the trilogy, the dark side warrior Kylo Ren, I would be able to connect with the part of JJ Abrams that had done the best he could.
And who was probably haunted by his own inner demons.

Just like Kylo Ren had been a victim of mental abuse since before birth, when a dark Lord invaded his mind and crushed his soul.
Kylo Ren never had a chance of staying on the right path.

And I was sure that in that light, the controversial choices of JJ Abrams too, could be explained by his deepest darkest fears getting the better of him.

Things that frightened him to the bone but that had been so terribly close, that he had been unable to separate them from his very own being.
Much less do anything about them.

And yet the intention to develop a more compassionate view of the man who had once given us the beautiful Star Wars 7,
including a bridal carry scene halfway through the movie and a bell in the first scene with Rey; both promises of a fairy tale,
did not bring out the wave of inspiration and healing I was hoping for.

On day six after seeing The Rise of Skywalker I was no way near forgiving him, for taking away our happy end.
For turning this into Romeo and Juliet, instead of Belle and the Beast.
But since I had announced on Twitter that I would be writing a compassionate review of The Rise of Starwalker, I felt the obligation to at least mention, that it was still on my mind, but that I could not find the right way to go about it.
So that's what I tweeted.

And one tweet turned into two.
Two into four.
And by now they had numbers followed by slash/ and the word "thread".

I knew I was on to something and that I had no idea how long this thread was going to be, or which story I was going to tell.

And this illustrates how I feel about writing and art;
In my opinion all you can do is let the story come out. It must reveal itself.

I'm sure writing a film script is in many ways different to blogging or tweeting, but having said that, I do believe that if I had been convinced, that for The Rise of Skywalker, JJ Abrams had been following his own inner-voice?

I would have wholeheartedly accepted it.

Even if The Rise of Skywalker had been about all of them turning to the dark side, and submerging the entire galaxy into darkness for eons to come;

If that's how JJ Abrams, director and screenplay writer, had seen this movie with great clarity?

Then so it shall be done.

The entire problem was: We never got that impression.

As far as I could see, something already went very wrong when the first director for this episode Colin Trevorrow was fired or resigned, based on creative differences.

This was before The Last Jedi was released, so it didn't have anything to do with Disney responding to disappointing box office results or anything.

Colin Trevorrow must have experienced a limitation that didn't allow him to make the film he wanted to make, but the film Disney wanted to make. His resignation should have been a red flag for JJ saying yes.

What exactly had he said yes to?

In the Twitter thread I'm sharing below, I've let this conflict play out with the character of Palpetine, because Trevorrow has always claimed his script did not include a return of the emperor.

The Emperor, came with JJ.

If I read the thread below, I can see I have not totally succeeded in my setup to write a non-salty review, that is compassionate to everyone involved. Technically, it is not even a review.

And I must say I am very sorry for that.
But I let the story out, as it wanted to come out.

And in the end?
That is really all any artist, any creator, any writer, and any filmmaker, can ever do.
Nothing more.
Nothing less.

~Lauren

A REYLO FAIRY TALE ON THE RISE OF SKYWALKER

Originally published as a thread on Twitter @LSHarteveld

I really wanted to write a compassionate piece on The Rise of Skywalker,

but my thoughts are all over the place.

I think about toxic masculinity a lot.

I can't write until I've found my inner Rose

*/

I'm a sequel-fan.

I really never "felt" Star Wars, until right before The Last Jedi:
I checked its spoiler reviews and encountered Reylo!

Suddenly the strange feeling I had felt after TFA made sense.

I rushed to the theater and never came back. Until now that is.

*/

I believe JJ did put the option of a love story into The Force Awakens.
But he didn't push it.

The strongest evidence is the care put into making Kylo a Disney
prince!

But JJ's TFA left too much room for interpretation, which caused
conflict between fans.

2/thread

So the two years after The Force Awakened a war was fought, between
early Reylos and fans of the originals and the prequels.

The Reylos were outnumbered.

No one believed their story that Rey from Jakku would fall for the dark
side warrior Kylo Ren.

3/thread

In December 2017 The Last Jedi was released.
Critics praised this character driven Star Wars movie, and the Reylos were over the moon!

Rey and Kylo Ren were going bring balance and save the universe by their union of the dark and light.

Until something happened..

4/thread

Fans of the prequels and the originals were furious.

Although once at war with each other, back in 1999 when the first prequel came out, they had now joined forces and they lashed out at the The Last Jedi, with anything that remotely looked like canon.

5/thread

They hit so hard Disney suffered financially, or at least they thought they had.

Or would. Or would in the future. Who knows what they thought.

As a response Disney ghosted Rian Johnson:
the same director whose film they had praised and had offered extra work.

6/thread

The Last Jedi haters also took their anger out on Reylos.

But by now they were with many.

The Force Awakens had been the spark but The Last Jedi set fire to the Reylo flame.

For two long years, Reylo fires burned bright on all social media.

7/thread

After The Force Awakened Reylos had been a minority.

But after the Last Jedi the groups were equal in size

And the Reylos used a weapon the antis did not understand:
The narrative.

Which means they were incredibly strong with the Force And they were winning

8/thread

But behind the scenes, in the final months before the release of the Last Jedi, something had happened that would change the fate of all Reylos.

A new man was appointed to direct final movie, of what Reylos considered "their" trilogy

And it would be their downfall.

9/thread

On a quest to bring the final chapter of the the saga back to the fans of the prequels and the originals, the new director forged an allegiance with a mighty foe:

The Emperor

The most powerful misogynist that had ever existed and the arch enemy of the Reylos.

10/thread

For two years the new director worked on his masterpiece:
One film, to rule them all.
One film, to bind them.

And while the world held its breath to the grand final of The Nine, The Emperor said his cooperation required one more thing.

A human sacrifice.

11/thread

The director could smell victory was near.

The fans of the prequels and originals were excited about the upcoming movie and Reylos were looking forward to see their ship sail to its final destination.

The war had stopped
For a brief moment there was peace in the galaxy

12/thread

"What sacrifice, my Lord?" the director asked.

As his mind went over who he could spare from his cast and crew.

The Emperor answered: "Bring me the heart of Kylo Ren."

The director was shocked.

"But my Lord, it is not mine to give. It belongs to Rey from Jakku."

13/thread

But the Emperor did not yield.

Months before the movie's release the director ripped the heart from Kylo Ren's chest and gave it to the Emperor.

Then he ordered the cast to return to set except for the actor who played Kylo Ren.
His services were no longer needed

14/thread

In the final months the director reshot 30% of all material, and feverishly edited his masterpiece.

But the actors had become quiet. They did what they were obliged to do, but no one talked about the movie or promoted it.

Their faces had become like masks.

15/thread

Rumors grew.

Stories that the director had sacrificed the heart of Kylo Ren reached the Reylos.

And while the fans of the prequels and the sequels uncorked their champagne and toasted to the return of the emperor, the Reylos refused to believe their hero had died.

16/thread

Timezone after timezone, Reylos around the world went to see the premiere of the movie.

And one by one they fell.

Because the rumors were right:
In sharp contrast to the happy end, as promised by the promotional material that had been released, Kylo Ren died.

17/thread

The Reylos had been betrayed.

Kylo Ren had been erased from the film, and just like Rey from Jakku – who ended up all alone on a desert planet exactly where she started – the Reylos too, were exactly where they started.
But they had learned an important lesson.

18/thread

The Reylos went their separate ways.

Some raised money for @AITAF, from the actor who had played Kylo Ren:

Others started #thankyourianjohnson, the Reylo patron saint

But not one Reylo ever spoke of what they learned.

Because some things are best forgotten.

19/THE END

A Reylo Fairy Tale on The Rise of Skywalker
was written on 24 December 2019

5

A FAREWELL TO A DARK SIDE WARRIOR

One of the things that struck me most, during this last month of the decade, is how I seem to have spent way more time processing The Rise of Skywalker, which presented me with the most unwelcome ending for the dark side warrior Kylo Ren, than I have processing the even more unwelcome breakup from my own dark sider.

Which in itself, gave reason for endless analysis, but by that time it had become a meta question:
"Why am I so not okay with a fictional character not getting his happily ever, and not with me, not getting my happily ever after?"

Not being okay with the ending Disney had for us, bore the hallmarks of a dirty breakup.
All I could think of was: WHY?!

WHY did you do this and that in (fill in Star Wars episode 7 or 8) and this and that in (fill in novelizations of 7 or 8)?

And why did this and this actor say such and such about the movie; Only to have it end this way?

Why does the final 30 minutes of the movie not have any dialogue for Kylo Ren?
Was it really that last minute?
After three years of production, you don't even have scenes with

dialogue that support the ending of your male protagonist?
So you just mute them and copy past the entire ending to a 40+ years saga?

Yet, I never asked any explanation to my lover as to why he did what he did. The thought didn't even cross my mind.
If anything, I offered an explanation to him.
During our 5 years together, he liked what I did for him. But it was something extra.
Like sugar or alcohol, or even a la carte dining at the finest restaurants. I was something that he would always enjoy and maybe even need at some points in his life, but he would never allow it to be the basis of his life.
So he never made the impression he wanted me to be anything more, because he didn't see a future where I played a role he understood.

I don't want to live together, nor get married.
I don't want to be seen as a couple, unless it's a super modern one, where people understand I am his equal. A woman who will win over his heart time and time again, and him a man who may spend time in your bed or your life.
If he stays with you, then good for you.
It was fair game and I lost.

But I'm not going to pretend to be the traditional woman next to a successful man. I'm not a trophy wife, nor a gold digger, nor am I half of a power couple who go to events together and are praised and admired by the other successful people around them.
The business man and his second wife, the writer.
Not going to happen, because then we become part of the people around us. We become owned, and I am free.

But I respect that he wants to play a bigger role, a more traditional one. He already had that when we met. I applaud that when he feels the

time has come to focus on that, and he wants to leave his mistress. "Goodbye. I will always love you, and miss you so much. But I understand, I really do."
Not:
"wHaT tHe fLyInG fUcK dID yoU Do tHAt FOr?!"

As disturbed as I was by Disney's ending, and what it meant in the grand scheme of things
- "Who was behind it? What purpose did it serve?" –
that's how easy I could let go when it was my own lover.

I have a couple of pages of notes next to me.
They cover a lot.
From all the plot holes in The Rise of Skywalker, to the symbolic meaning of The Emperor, the symbolism of killing off a dark and conflicted character who is loved by the female heroine.
The notes speak of ways in which Kylo Ren/ Ben Solo could come back, because the world where he died, Exogol, is part of the World Between Worlds.
The rules of life and death do not apply there.

There are many notes, but in the end I think the only purpose they really served was for me to understand we are never entitled to happy endings.
Not even if it's Disney, let alone real life.
That people may or may not come back.
But that the most important thing is that you let them go, when they have to leave.
And never stop loving them.

A Farewell to a Dark side Warrior
was written on 28 December 2019

6

THE DESERT GODDESS

This is a letter to my creativity coach Sara.
Before our call I always give her a headsup.

Dear Sara,

Every time I write you, I feel like checking what I wrote last time. As if I fear you are keeping checklists of my analysis and conclusions, my plans and resolutions. When in the highly unlikely case that you did, I know you would never use them against me.

That I don't have to meet any standards of consistency, although obviously a part of me still thinks investing in creativity coaching requires some sort of accountability.

I went to Star Wars 9 and to my unpleasant surprise the leaks were true.

Despite its promising part 7 and 8, the entire sequel saga which started in 2015, was not about a love story between the dark side warrior Kylo Ren and his equal in the light, the girl from Jakku.

It was about the birth of an overpowered super heroine (the antis use this as something bad, but I've decided to claim that as my bio) who doesn't need anybody.

Or at least I hope so, because she ended up all alone without the love of her life, on a desert planet to, as Twitter put it;

"eat sand."

You can't blame Star Wars for lack of symbolism, when they let her love interest (who was still on the dark side then) snatch a fertility necklace from her neck, through Force projection.

I thought this was subliminal messaging for some kind of reference to rough sex.

But apparently it meant:

"No sex for you.

Stay a virgin and if you're lucky we'll give you an immaculate conception so that we can keep fantasizing about you and we don't have to compete with tall, dark and handsome warriors."

Eat sand, check.

Just like Rey's future had suddenly changed from happily ever after with her dark prince to facing life alone, my future changed to when my own tall and handsome lover called it quits.

And just like Rey, I tried to tell myself I would get over it, there were more fish in the sea (although few in the desert), and it would all be a chance to redesign my love life.

Being a mistress had been unsatisfactory with regard to the number of times I had sex. I had not had sex for 5 month when we broke up. Which was an advantage when processing the breakup, but in previous years the numbers had been modest as well.

I could see how becoming fully single, would help me to adjust to the idea of having multiple men in my life.

But only when I'm in love.

The major takeaway from having been single since 2006, has been that I know that sex without being in love is just as boring to me, as sex within a long-term relationship where the passion has died out.

This requirement alone may very well be why I might never have sex again and I'm okay with that.

So I was left alone with my thoughts on how I could use this time as a single to upgrade my sex life from having the basics/ a mindset in place that could support one lover, to one that supported at least the idea of having two lovers.

But against any and all of my expectations, something happened that was the opposite of what I expected;
When I masturbated my orgasms had intensified.
Practically overnight.
The first time was two days after the breakup.
It was a session of which I thought:
"Let's get this over with, so that I have that first time out of the way," and BOOM!

The only time I remember experiencing this, was around 2006; When I was in my early 30s.
I had always assumed it had been an age thing.
At that age your body does what it can to talk you into making babies. But with the same thing happening now, it's much more likely it was sparked by me and my partner breaking up!
Just like now, it was a very smooth breakup, nothing dramatic.
We even stayed together, living together for another two years. As friends.

So apparently, as much time as I had invested in figuring out my sexuality and my relationships, as much as I had gained knowledge over all those years –
I know who I am right now, and that I had been right in 2006 that a long-term sexual relationship really was not my thing-
I had overlooked something major as well:
That I was absolutely fine, being alone.
If anything, I was doing better.

I will never stop loving tall, dark and handsome warriors.

And still think Rey and her man should have ended up together, they deserved it.

But as far as my own sex life goes, I now know that there really is no reason whatsoever to "invest" in a love life or to turn myself inside out in order to be able to deal with two lovers.

In the end I am just as happy alone in the desert.
And certainly just as hot.

The Desert Goddess
was written on 29 December 2019

7

HAPPILY EVER AFTER (HEA) WAS MORE IMPORTANT IN STAR WARS THAN IN MARRIAGE STORY

"Many women feel like they have wasted their time buying into a franchise that ultimately never cared about fulfilling its own promises about happy endings,
telling a complete story, or even offering hope and compassion to the characters that needed it the most."

Quoted from
"Star Wars: Why Reylo Outrage Inspired #ReleaseTheJJCut"

I just got back from seeing Marriage Story, and it left me a bit sore.

I had assumed that because people were so enthusiastic about this movie, the couple played by Adam Driver and Scarlett Johansson would ultimately get back together after their divorce process gets from bad to worse.

I had gone to the movies because I longed to see Adam Driver on the big screen, and had vowed not to see The Rise of Skywalker anymore.

The Rise of Skywalker, TROS, was 2019;
This was the new year and it was not invited.

So instead of breaking my resolution for a TROS-free decade, I went to see Wedding Story, also with Adam Driver. I have skipped The Report because that was too serious and heavy for me, but Marriage Story was doable.

Like I said, all the positive feedback for this movie had convinced me there was much to like, and probably included a happy end.
After all, it was called Marriage Story.
Making it painfully obvious that I had learned very little from Rise of Skywalker, which should have been called *The Rise of Palpetine*.
But hey! That does not sell!
Neither does a movie called *Divorce Story*.

So I went to the movies, chose Marriage Story, and I was disappointed.

In Dutch we have an expression that allows you to say something is "a dragon of a movie".
It was as if I was watching a Woody Allen movie, and I'd rather not.

I read people thought the director of Marriage Story created movies that looked a lot like Woody Allen's, because they revolve around relationships and New York. But I think them and me differ on whether that's a good thing or a dragon of a movie.

So either way, Marriage Story was (for me) almost unbearable to watch. There was no reason for these people to get a divorce other than that they both brought so many unspoken expectations into that marriage, it was simply doomed to fail unless they were going to talk about it.

Which apparently they could not without getting very angry with each other.

Neither one of the parties was taking any responsibility for not setting any boundaries and goals of their own during their marriage and had just plunged into the deep end hoping for the best.

Which turned out to become a very nasty and very expensive divorce ten years later.

And then there are moments when they could have seen how easy it was to love each other, and that it is all a big misunderstanding and yet they don't see anything!

As the viewer you can see the potential is still there, yet apparently they experience it as a cathartic cry and still go through with the divorce.
It made no sense.

So on my way home I started pondering if I needed to write about this movie Marriage Story.
And if so, what was I going to write?

Ultimately I decided I was going write about it in conjunction with The Rise of Skywalker.

Both movies had ended on a bad note, in particular for the character Adam Driver had played.
But Marriage Story had received raving reviews.

Whereas The Rise of Skywalker had mixed reviews from critics and Rotten Tomatoes shut down the pole to prevent its audience review would go down. It's had the same audience score for two weeks.

So I started thinking about this critically acclaimed Woody Allen-like divorce drama, which was loved by the audience and not by me; Versus the critically not acclaimed Rise of Skywalker movie, which was also not loved by the audience nor by me.

Although many disgruntled fans still wanted to make the point TROS was "Way better than The Last Jedi!"

To understand what that means, we must go down and search Star Wars at its roots, take a meta perspective on the origins of the latest trilogy.
Why for people like me, The Rise of Skywalker was not just a bad movie in particular in comparison to The Last Jedi;
But also why people like me are invested in Star Wars in a way that does not even begin to compare with seeing a one-off Woody Allen-like movie.

To understand why a movie like Marriage Story will never get my heart, nor any other heart like mine, pumped with excitement or broken from grief, we need to go back to 2015.

To a movie called The Force Awakens, which was the first part of the new trilogy also known as "The Sequel trilogy".
And we need to establish that this movie, nor its successor The Last Jedi was an accident.
But that they belonged to a story that was set out by Disney for this trilogy.

A story that was abandoned.

As was the group of new fans that had embraced it as their own:
The group of people, known as Reylos.

THE STORY OF THE REYLOS

For over 2,5 weeks I have been glued to my Twitter timeline, reading everything about the heavily disappointing Star Wars 9 The Rise of Skywalker.
My addiction ultimately paid off in giving me The Ultimate Article on Everything Wrong with The Rise of Skywalker.

It was titled:
"Star Wars: Why Reylo Outrage Inspired #ReleaseTheJJCut"

This article pleads for release of the original/ real ending, by JJ Abrams.
And although the title does not fully cover it, the article sums up everything wrong with Star Wars 9, in particular from a Reylo perspective.

I will explain in a minute why that is defendable as the most relevant perspective.
But let me first explain what "Reylo" means.
It stands for the relationship between Rey and Kylo Ren.

Their love story roots in the myth of Death and the Maiden, in the Phantom of the Opera and it is almost a direct clone of Disney's other favorite (Star Wars is owned by Disney), Belle and the Beast.

The Beast, Death or the Phantom was Kylo Ren, played by the tallest actor of his generation Adam Driver, who has made it big with numerous highly acclaimed movies.
Adam Driver played Kylo Ren, Disney's dark prince, who would be united with his equal in the light, the girl Rey from Jakku.

Together Rey and Kylo would bring balance to The Force:

The dark side warrior with the light inside of him and the light side warrior Rey with the dark inside of her. Like the black yin and light yang, both having one dot of the other inside of them.

Oh!

Now that I am unapologetically making Kylo Ren "Yin", which is also the female element, I am reminded of an interesting perspective which was offered on Twitter directly, so I don't have an article (yet?), about how the tall handsome warrior Kylo Ren is actually portrayed as very feminine.

Not only does he possess the long flowy Disney prince hair;
He also uses his voice, his eyes, his mystery to seduce her.
At one point he's shirtless when he talks to her, throwing Rey off as she stammers if he perhaps has a cowl to cover himself up.

For me it were indeed these feminine aspects that made Kylo irresistible.

So Reylos, or Reylo shippers are the people who "ship" (from relationship) the pairing of Rey and Kylo.
A pairing which – and this is important in the light of where things went – was setup and supported by Disney themselves.

As much as more traditional Star Wars fans may argue otherwise, episode 7 The Force Awakens (2015) and in particular episode 8 The Last Jedi (2017) were setting up a story that was more sexual, sensual, spiritual and more mythical, than any of the previous Star Wars movies had ever been.

If the third trilogy was rooted in anything from the past, it was much more in the Prequels;
A series of movies George Lucas himself made at the beginning of this

century. And at the time, the prequels were heavily criticized by the fans of the originals.

Fans of the originals did not like the prequel trilogy.
And now both fans of the originals and fans of the prequels, didn't like the theme of the sequels.

But here is how it differs and where the recent criticism turned into the downfall of the entire sequel trilogy:
Because in the case of the prequels, the criticism never got to influence the story.
George Lucas knew the bigger story and he stuck with it.

But what happened in the sequels is that episode 7 was different, fresh, but not too different. And was still ambiguous with regard to the love theme. It was this ambiguity that ensured the older fanbase liked it, and drew in the first of the new fanbase.

The Reylo shippers.

But then came 8, The Last Jedi.

The romantic story was dialed up and all hell broke loose.
Criticism was usually not directly aimed at the romance, nor at the socially conscious themes 8 had included.
Instead it was projected at what was "done to" Luke Skywalker (he was a bitter man regretting the choices he had made, instead of a Jedi superhero), and on how many or more how few lightsaber fights 8 had.

But the point that should have been made then, is that those complaints were entirely irrelevant to the bigger story which was being told.
The story that after hiding in episode 7, was finally becoming more explicit and more visible.

And if George Lucas had done this trilogy, just like he had done the prequels, he would have held the course.

He would not have changed the story, because of nitpicking on choices that didn't have anything to do with the bigger narrative.

But as the old Star Wars fans were angry because they saw Star Wars canon, and the characters as they saw them, being compromised in 8, Disney grew uncomfortable with the path they had chosen.

There are people pointing out that Disney has creative freedom, and that it's okay for these three movies of the final trilogy to have an entirely different tone;

There are even those wondering if Reylos have a right to ask or expect a Happily Ever After.

Yes, we do.

Not because that is what "we" want to see, but because that is what has been fed to us.

THAT is the story Disney set up, that is the entire thing this sequel trilogy is based on. Or was based on, until they first got cold feet after the backlash from the Last Jedi.

And then weeks before the premiere they got cold all the way up to the waistline, because they changed the entire ending.

The ending of The Rise of Skywalker does not contain any original material of Adam Driver "acting" his death.

They used material, in all likeliness from his Happily Ever After, and edited it using every dirty trick in the book, until it looked like he had died

And Rey – who had been hailed during the entire movie as being half of "A dyad in the Force! A power like life itself! Unseen for generations!" was copied from her Pasaana shots, and pasted into

Tatooine.
Alone.

And voila!
Disney's half of the Dyad, also known as Belle, is now redubbed to Wonder Woman in space, and doesn't need anybody anymore.
There was no footage of her mourning the dead side of her dyad, her other half, and the man with whom she had been having heated Force conversations with for over a year;

Instead they let her commemorate his mother Leia and his uncle, Luke Skywalker with whom she had a difficult relationship.
Just like Adam Driver didn't do any acting for his ending, this footage too was most likely entirely fabricated and the actress who played Rey never got a chance to act as someone who had just lost her soulmate.
They just copy pasted her into the desert.

Rey in the final minutes of the film, has been compared to the Stepford Wives:
She does not show any emotion only an artificial smile.

BAD ENDINGS

I feel Star Wars was never for me.
Or, as the article said it:

> *"Star Wars has the bitter taste of a franchise that accidentally tapped into women's interests but had little interest in them as intelligent viewers engaging with the material."*

Quote from:
Star Wars: Why Reylo Outrage Inspired #ReleaseTheJJCut

We were lured in with the promise of an epic fairy tale, and then we were kicked out that we should be strong, be alone and eat sand.

That made Star Wars 9, The Rise of Skywalker, so painful for me and all the other Reylos.
We thought the story would transcend our pain and suffering, and provide healing.

Yet I would never bring those kinds of expectations to a real life.
Not into a real life relationship between a man and a woman.

The reason Marriage Story never really got to me, is that even I, a romantic Reylo, know that expectations of your other half completing you, do not belong in a marriage.

They were a thing Disney fed us.

A long long time ago.

Happily ever after (HEA) was more important in Star Wars than in Marriage Story
was written on 5 January 2020

THIS BOOK

As I am editing this, it is strange for me to reread this book;
A collection of deeply personal posts that described how important the sequel trilogy was for me, in what was probably the darkest time of my life.
The first post is written on 28 January 2018, a little over two weeks after my cat Max died, who had been suffering from explainable an unexplainable ailments since spring 2016.
Our relationship had become symbiotic.

2017 Had been an emotional year, as my best friend migrated to the United States.
And now there I was, December, holiday season. I knew it would be the last one Max would be with me, and I took care of him in every way I could.
By then he only ate chicken that had been cooked for 8 hours.

December 2017 was also the month The Last Jedi came out, and I impulse-attended it, on a moment I could leave Max alone.
I was blown away, and fell in love with the dark side warrior Kylo Ren.
I went to see it again and again, and brought all my friends there, and if they didn't know Star Wars I would give a 30 minute-crash course in the lobby of cinema, so that they went in prepared.
I had a notebook with me, where I drew out diagrams that explained family ties, relationships, who was who;
An overview of the most important locations, and an introduction to the first 10-15 minutes of the movie, which I always found the most difficult part of The Last Jedi, because it was about the evacuation of a rebel base on a planet, and a fight in the galaxy above.

In total I saw The Last Jedi 8 times in the theater, in the final weeks around Max's death.

One of the things I did to prepare myself for the grief of his death, was think how I would comfort myself. What could I do or buy?
I decided I would buy a little Kylo Ren doll I had come across on eBay.
It said things like:
"Don't fight it, you know you can't."
"I've been waiting for this day for a long time."
And:
"I'm immune to the light"
The last line never made it to the movie, just to the doll.
Just like "But I do" never made it to The Rise Of Skywalker, and was only in a trailer.

After Max died, 12 January 2018, I ordered the Kylo Ren doll who became my companion. I also bought The Force Awakens on dvd and when The Last Jedi came out on dvd I bought that one too.
Just like other fans, I had my eyes on the horizon, on December 2019 when the last installment of the trilogy would premiere.
It would also be the month my love relationship ended.

It is around those moments, early 2018 and December 2019, that these diary entries and stories were written.
And rereading them, I think it is safe to say having this topic, this interest, and something to hold on to for two years, is what got me through.
The Star Wars sequel trilogy and the talking Kylo Ren doll, saved me.

May the Force be with you.
Always.

Lauren Harteveld
18 August 2021

All books available worldwide at:

https://www.lulu.com/spotlight/LaurenandLulu

THE WAIT WORTH 8 (2017)

1. **Mango**, een novelle *Dutch*
   Seksuele safari, van de jaren '80 tot de zero's.

2. **Dutch American Diary** (2008-2009)
   Lauren is in love with two men;
   One cunning wizard and one half her age.
   ~Dutch American Diary part 1

3. **22 Erotische Verhalen** *Dutch*
   Literaire pornografie in de geest van Anais Nin
   en Isabel Allende.

4. **LS Diary** (2012-2013)
   About three dark men and Lauren getting naked on stage.
   Not necessarily together.
   ~Dutch American Diary part 2

5. **De Candystop** (2013) *Dutch*
   Waar de Nederlandse literatuur tot stilstand komt door een
   Marokkaanse lekkernij.

6. **Bedtime Stories** (2014)
   Facing her demons and her muse, Lauren's sexual history
   gets its worthy finale.
   ~Dutch American Diary part 3

7. **Mirage** (2014)
   Giving you a little dessert, with all gorgeous writers from
   previous books.
   ~Dutch American Diary epilogue

8. **Big**, diaries and erotica (2015-2016)
   The crown to Lauren's life; a secret affair with her Biggie.

SEPARATE BOOKS

These books are not part of the numbered (diary) series

- **Het Boek Benjamin** *Dutch and English*
  Collected works, contains book 1 -8 from the previous page

- **Witte Tijgerin**, *Dutch*
  Gids voor solitaire vrouwen die een geweldig seksleven
  willen en plenty energie.

- **The White Tigress Yoga Workbook**

- **The Mistress Speaks** (2018 - 2021)
  Channeling a lost archetype

- **The Beach, C.** (2018 - 2021)
  Diary, letters and essays inspired by Basic Instinct's
  Catherine Tramell

- **Star Wars is finally telling women *cross out***
  everybody to start enjoying The Thing (2018 - 2019)
  And other deeply personal blogposts about the sequel trilogy
  that did not age well

www.ingramcontent.com/pod-product-compliance
Lightning Source LLC
Chambersburg PA
CBHW070513220526